The Arena of Truth:
The Trouble with Truth

I0190248

By Bob Mumford

LIFECHANGERS®

P.O. Box 3709 ❖ Cookeville, TN 38502
931.520.3730 ❖ lc@lifechangers.org

Bob Sutton's editing was instrumental in helping me put together the pieces of this Plumbline. Bob nurtures the body of Christ as a pastor and educator. He served many years as an editor of *New Wine* magazine. I would like to express my gratitude for his friendship and his assistance with *The Arena of Truth*.

Unless otherwise noted, all Scripture quotations are taken from *The New American Standard Bible*, The Lockman Foundation, 1960, 1962, 1963, 1968, 1972, 1973, 1975, 1977. All rights reserved.

PLUMBLINE

Published by:

LIFECHANGERS ®
L I B R A R Y S E R I E S

P.O. Box 3709 | Cookeville, TN 38502
(800) 521-5676 | www.lifechangers.org

The Arena of Truth:
The Trouble with Truth

By Bob Mumford

Truth is troublesome. Alexander Solzhenitsyn opened his Harvard 1978 commencement address with these words:

> Many of you have already found out, and others will find out in the course of their lives, that truth eludes us if we do not concentrate our attention totally on its pursuit. But even while it eludes us, the illusion of knowing it still lingers and leads to many misunderstandings. Also, truth seldom is pleasant; it is almost invariably bitter. There is some bitterness in my today's speech too, but I want to stress that it comes not from an adversary, but from a friend.

I know of few men who approach truth with as much insight as Alexander Solzhenitsyn. He apprehended truth in a most violent arena—the oppression of Communist Russia. His address to the Harvard graduates was a moral inditment of the "spiritual exhaustion" of Western culture. The truth he presented was not about the validity of social or economic theories but about our spiritual integrity and the 20th century's moral poverty. In this brief quote, he makes three most insightful statements about truth, which in some ways succinctly summarize why truth is so troublesome:

First, truth is elusive and requires active pursuit. As we continue the study of the arena of truth[1], it is not facts and theories we are pursuing. We seek a moral and spiritual alignment with reality in God.

Second, he says in some strange way we hold with certainty to the belief we possess the truth. This can lead us to a misunderstanding of reality.

Third, genuine truth is most often unpleasant and even bitter when encountered in the arena.

When truth comes to us, it is often something we don't want to hear. Your pastor says, "I think you may have a problem with your temper." And you get mad. Truth is threatening you. Please remember truth as we are trying to lay hold of it, is not about debatable facts. Truth, as we will encounter it, is the spiritual reality that governs the Universe and each of our lives. This is why the Bible teaches us to learn how to love truth. We experience the full extent of our salvation in the love and acceptance of truth.[2] If we love truth, we learn how to embrace it even when it appears negative. Truth contains the path to our freedom.

Having said that, I want to quickly add that truth can often bring joy and freedom in its first

1 The first volume, *The Arena of Truth: Establishing the Borders*, is available at www.lifechangers.org
2 See 2 Thess. 2:10.

appearance. Do you remember the first time you really understood your sins were forgiven? That you are secure in God's care? That God will be faithful to bring about the best for your life? Once truth becomes reality for us, it ultimately brings freedom and joy. Some of these realities come to us by sheer grace. They ensure us of the steadfastness of our covenantal relationship with the Father through Christ. The negative aspect of truth is our reaction to the things the Lord brings to our attention because they hinder our fellowship with Him.

Why do we resist the truth that God sends to set us free? What makes it appear negative? Jesus explains:

> This is the judgment, that the Light has come into the world, and men loved the darkness rather than the Light, for their deeds were evil. For everyone who does evil hates the Light and does not come to the Light for fear that his deeds will be exposed. But he who practices the truth comes to the Light, so that his deeds may be manifested as having been wrought in God.[3]

Humanity loves darkness rather than the light because their deeds are evil. While in the Navy I spent an inordinate amount of time in bars. Bars

---

3 John 3:19-21

tend to be dark. Why? People want to go there and not necessarily be known. Darkness is acceptable and welcome in that environment. When do most burglaries occur? In the darkness the burglar has a covering for his evil intentions.

By contrast, light has a very powerful effect on its environment. You can sit at a table that looks clean, but if the sun pours in through the window, every speck of dust on the table becomes obvious. You can even see specs of dust floating around in the air because the sunlight reveals everything that might not normally be seen. Darkness makes everybody comfortable, but when the light comes everything is revealed.

We might be quick to say, "Oh, Lord, we want to know truth!" But when the Lord brings it to us, it may be something we don't want to hear. The Lord sees things as they really are. When we are happy and spiritual, listening to our favorite TV preacher tell us how blessed we are, we can become spiritually "anesthetized." But when God brings us into the truth of reality it can be brutal.

One day I was walking along feeling all spiritual, and I said to the Lord, "Lord, show me to me," and He did! The blinding light of reality revealed things concealed and covert that I had so cleverly hidden from others, and even to some degree, from myself. I ended up on my knees, devastated and sobbing. This must be why Paul tells us that the Lord dwells in "unapproachable light."[4] Since then, I have preferred the Lord to grant me light in smaller measures.

I want to give you three basic things we must understand about truth if we are to successfully engage the arena:

1. Truth is a Person

Truth, as we are understanding it, is not an abstract idea or set of facts. It is a person. Jesus said, "I am the Truth."[5] Truth in the Old Testament is God, and truth in the New Testament is our Lord Jesus Christ. To begin to understand this is more important than we can possibly imagine. We have been trained through our Western culture to approach truth like Greek philosophers. The Greeks taught us to approach truth as something abstract, separated from reality. Truth was a set of concepts that could be placed in a little fanciful box and be manipulated according to human imagination.

Please notice in the passage cited above Jesus says, "He who *practices* the truth." In Scripture, truth always has to do with *reality* and *the action that parallels it.* This is most important as it affects our fellowship with the Lord. The Apostle John tells us, "If we say that we have fellowship with Him and yet walk in the darkness, we lie and do not *practice the truth*."[6] John does *not say*, "Believe the truth."

4 1 Timothy 6:16
5 John 14:6
6 1 John 1:6 [emphasis added]

In the Eastern biblical worldview, belief was never separated from behavior as in our Western manner of thinking. This is why a church may have a wonderful statement of faith (beliefs) and still manifest ungodly attitudes and hateful behavior. Remember that in the years following the Reformation, Christians who sought purity of doctrine (correct Biblical beliefs) also persecuted and slaughtered one another.

God is always consistent with Himself. In other words, God always acts in a manner that manifests the reality of who He is. Truth and action in God could be compared to a railroad track. If you look down a railroad, the tracks appear to come together. However, we know they continue parallel to each other no matter how far we follow them. If the track curves, both tracks curve together, always the same distance apart. God is like that as illustrated here by the two parallel arrows. We need to emphasize again that truth, as we are using it here, is not an abstract set of concepts to which God conforms. When we speak of truth in relation to God we speak of His being and His person. He is Truth. His actions are always consistent with His being.

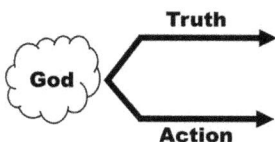

If I am belaboring this, it is intentional. As we progress into the arena, we will continually discover that the purpose of God for all creation and for each of us is to be brought back into alignment with the truth of His being. Once the implications of this begin to settle into our understanding, our calling in Christ ceases to be merely personal and becomes cosmic in scope.

2. Truth is Eternal and Fixed

Truth is eternal and fixed. In other words, God is the same for everybody, at all times, in all cultures, in every age of redemptive history. Even though He accommodates our human limitations, He does not change who He is on our behalf. "Jesus Christ, is the same yesterday, today and forever."[7] He reveals Himself throughout Scripture as the eternal I AM. He says to His disciples, "I am the Way, the Truth, and the Life."[8]

Because truth is fixed and eternal, we know how He will deal with us in the future:

> He has fixed a day in which He will judge the world in righteousness through a Man whom He has appointed, having furnished proof to all men by raising Him from the dead.[9]

The importance of this statement will become even more important shortly. We will see that because Jesus perfectly conformed Himself to the truth as the Son of Man, He is qualified to judge humanity as one who has lived as a man. Judgment

7 Hebrews 13:8
8 John 14:6
9 Acts 17:31

will not be made by some abstract set of rules but by one who has conformed himself to truth—the nature of God.

3. Truth Demands Reality

Paul writes to the Galatians, "Have I become your enemy by telling you the truth?"[10] The Galatian church had departed from the truth of the Gospel, and Paul was writing to save them from slipping into spiritual bondage. He was confronting them with the reality of the danger they were in.

The arena of truth has been designed by God to confront us with reality. However, reality is difficult to embrace. Most of Paul's epistles were written to bring the churches into the reality of Christ and His Kingdom. He wrote to the Ephesians:

> We are no longer to be children, tossed here and there by waves and carried about by every wind of doctrine, by the trickery of men, by craftiness in deceitful scheming; but *speaking the truth in love*, we are to grow up in all aspects into Him who is the head, even Christ.[11] [Emphasis added].

Paul is describing what is today called spin. News outlets spin their coverage of the news to substantiate the version of "reality" they want you

10 Galatians 4:16
11 Ephesians 4:14-15

to believe. Paul says that if we are to grow up into maturity in Christ, who is the Truth and the Reality, we must speak about reality with each other. To be truthful with one another can be very difficult, but it is most necessary if the body of Christ is to mature.

God is Predictable, Dependable, and Consistent

Because God always acts according to His nature, we can say three things about Him. These may seem elementary and self-evident, but we will be using them to illustrate something exceedingly important as we look more closely at maturing in fellowship, the image of the Son, freedom, rulership, and fruitfulness.

Predictable. This is not to say that God will not act in unexpected ways, but there is little doubt about the overall actions of God toward humankind or us as individuals. His love never fails.

Dependable. Being able to depend on the faithfulness of God is foundational to our hope, trust, and faith.

Consistent. James tells us there is no "variation or shifting shadow"[12] in God. He will never relate or act in a manner that is inconsistent with His nature.

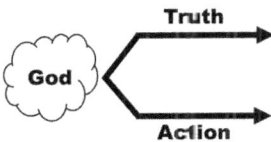

Let's look at an illustration of the first pair. Adam and Eve, created in the image of God, would have been predictable, dependable, and consistent

12 James 1:17

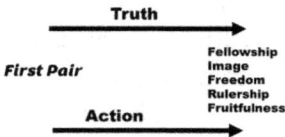

with the truth of God's nature. The image of God was more than a "look alike" image. The first pair were inseminated with God's spiritual DNA. Out of their fellowship, pictured as eating from the Tree of Life, they would rule creation in freedom and fruitfulness.

All humanity is affected by sin in the fall. When we talk about sin we most often associate it with things like immorality, stealing, cheating, cursing, etc. However, Ernest Williams, who for many years was general superintendent of the Assemblies of God, gave a definition of sin that was insightful and amazingly practical: "sin causes us to break down when God and others need us the most."

This is not a Biblical or theological definition, but a very practical one that fits our discussion. It takes us out of the moral and legal understanding of sin, which is valid and needed, and puts it in a practical context that fits the conflict of the arena.

As illustrated above, the first pair in the Garden had: fellowship, image, freedom, rulership, and fruitfulness. When sin came in through

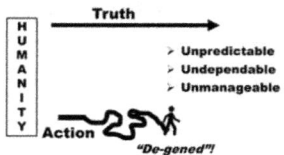

deception and disobedience, they were no longer able to walk in the truth. Something very basic in their spiritual genetic structure was corrupted. The history which follows in the next eleven chapters of Genesis is essentially the degeneration of human culture. Degeneration comes from two Latin words that mean "to move away from your birth." In other words, humanity moved further and further away from the spiritual DNA of the image of God. We were *"de-gened"!*

Until recently, genetically inherited physical defects and the tendency toward certain diseases have been largely incurable. Symptoms were treated, but the genetic problem remained. However, since the mapping of the human genome the possibility of altering defects within the genetic structure may offer the hope for a reversal. We will apply this to our spiritual DNA as we proceed.

Considering the above definition of sin, here are three simple words that describe the effects of sin on our actions, both internal and external.

First, sin makes us **unpredictable**. One moment a commuter on his way to work stops on the freeway to help a lady change her tire. Then he curses and flips off the guy who just cut him off in traffic. James warns us that out the same mouth comes both blessing and cursing.[13]

Second, sin makes us **undependable.** In other words, when it comes time for someone to depend on you, you may be off wandering or doing something on your own.

Third, sin makes us **inconsistent**. At times we find ourselves in a place where we fail to obey the

---

13 See James 3:10

Holy Spirit's leading or the voice of our redeemed conscience. I believe the most graphic description of the fruits of sin is given by Paul in Romans 7. Hear Paul's frustration from these excerpts:

> For what I am doing, I do not understand; for I am not practicing what I would like to do, but I am doing the very thing I hate. . . So now, no longer am I the one doing it, but sin which dwells in me. . . for the willing is present in me, but the doing of the good is not. For the good that I want, I do not do, but I practice the very evil that I do not want.
>
> I find then the principle that evil is present in me, the one who wants to do good. For I joyfully concur with the law of God in the inner man, but I see a different law in the members of my body, waging war against the law of my mind and making me a prisoner of the law of sin which is in my members. Wretched man that I am! Who will set me free from the body of this death?[14]

Paul found himself in the natural man to be *unpredictable, undependable, and inconsistent.* Through fellowship, Jesus longs to conform us to His

14 Romans 7:15; 17; 19; 21-24

image. We are to become dependable, predictable, and consistent. Can you imagine how different families and the Church would act if these three qualities were genuinely cultivated and practiced?

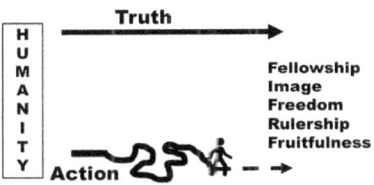

What is going to bring our wandering back to walking in conformity with the truth as represented by the arrow? First is the work of Jesus Christ. Then, our willingness to embrace truth in the arena is what will bring us back to walking consistently in the truth toward Father's ultimate purposes. However, there is always potential for us to continue to wander along on our own way. As we discussed in part one, our relationship with the Lord will remain secure, but we may never come to freedom and fruitfulness in God's kingdom.

We can be a person everybody loves but not be trustworthy. We may need more references before hiring some Christians than someone from the world. They may really love the Lord, but that's not the issue. Israel was secure in their covenant with the Lord, His chosen people. But when He asked them to enter and take the Land, they proved to be unpredictable and undependable. They refused to align themselves with the totality of God's revealed truth for them. They lost their inheritance.

Encountering the Arena

Truth comes to us in many guises, most of which we do not initially recognize as something we are being challenged to embrace. There are times when the truth brings us new freedom and joy. Can you remember the first time you really understood the Gospel? Or when you realized the completeness of your forgiveness? Or felt the Father's unqualified love for you? This is why Jesus said the truth would set us free!

However, as we begin to emerge from the deception and darkness of sin, the truth (especially what we most need to hear) can be negative and sometimes offensive at first appearance. I am not exaggerating when I say that how we respond can make the difference between fulfillment and stagnation in God's purposes.

First, I will illustrate the place of the arena in Father's purposes. Then I will unfold the different possible responses to the arena when we are required to enter it. Before I do, however, let me warn you that you are most likely already in an arena of some kind. You may or may not recognize it or perhaps you do. Either way, if you will fearlessly embrace the concepts we are unpacking, they will radically revolutionize your understanding of yourself and of how the Father is working to bring you to maturity in Christ. I have watched these realities play out over decades of ministry in some of the most painful instances including in my own person.

Jesus, as the Pattern Son

Let's look first at the life of Jesus since He is the Pattern Son whom we are invited to follow. Jesus never deviated in acting or responding in alignment with the truth of His Father. He was in tune with the Father and able to say, "I am *the Truth*." His life and actions were always consistent with what he taught. Looking at our illustration:

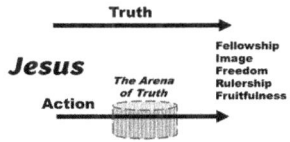

- He had unbroken *fellowship* with His Father.
- He was the "*image* of the invisible God".
- He knew complete *freedom* from sin, the fear of men, or the pressure to conform.
- He exercised *rulership* over the powers of darkness, the forces of nature, sickness, and deception.
- The *fruitfulness* of His life, death, and resurrection continues to multiply beyond measure to this day.

Now, here is the million-dollar question. Was it necessary for Jesus to encounter the conflict of the arena of truth?

Hear the testimony of Scripture:

- He was to become "the firstborn of many."
- "In all things He had to be made like His brethren."
- "He learned obedience from the things which He suffered."

- "Who has been tempted in all things as we are."
- God perfected "the author of their salvation through sufferings."[15]

Beyond these direct statements, there is Jesus' temptation by Satan in the wilderness. He entered the wilderness led by the Holy Spirit and exited the wilderness in the power of the Spirit. I think it is fair to surmise that as a result of His conflict with Satan, something matured in the person of the man Jesus. He unswervingly aligned Himself with the truth of God. He was predictable, dependable, and consistent.

Jesus encountered the arena, and He now lives to lead each of us through the arenas we encounter. As He faced the choices of His arenas, He always aligned Himself with the truth. He is thus qualified to come to our aid as we are tested. He was tested in all things without missing the mark of walking in fellowship and truth with His father. Even though He was not hampered by sin as we are, I do not believe His tests were any less real.

Jesus had an overarching focus and motivation that guided His every action and response. Out of His deepest being, He desired to please His father. "I always," He said, "do the things that are pleasing to Him."[16] He was not motivated by a set of rules or fulfilling a particular role. *His motivation was*

15 See Rom 8:29; Heb. 2:17; Heb. 5:8; Heb. 4:15; Heb. 2:10
16 John 8:29

relational—to love and please His father. Every decision He made, everything He said, every act He performed, and everything He suffered was focused on His pleasing His Father. We will do well to take this to heart in the challenges we face.

Paul, as an Example

As best as we know, Paul is an example of a person who was violently confronted with truth and embraced it. One day he was zealously persecuting the church on his way to Damascus when Jesus knocked him flat, spoke to him in a rather threatening manner, and left him blind. It is worth noting that the more religiously zealous we are, the more extreme the Lord may have to be to get our attention. That does not apply to everyone, but it is worth keeping in mind when life becomes chaotic.

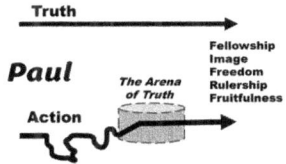

Once Paul laid hold of God's truth for his life, he became consistently aligned with the revealed truth. Paul was "re-gened" by the Spirit of Christ as he vividly expressed in Romans 8. Paul's motivation, like Jesus', for facing life's conflicts and suffering was love.[17] Paul aligned himself with a *Person*, the Lord Jesus. He was willing to "suffer the loss of all things" simply to know Him.[18] It was not a new <u>understanding</u> of scripture that motivated Paul. Paul

17 See 2 Cor. 5:14
18 See Phil. 3:8-10

was driven by a relationship.

Paul was so matured by his arena that Jesus entrusted him to carry the Gospel to the Gentile world and help set the course for the newborn church among the nations. He could be trusted. He had become dependable, predictable, and consistent. When the Lord spoke, Paul was there to do the Lord's bidding.

What About Us?

The Father desires to take us from where we are when He encounters us to being part of His "family business." With this goal in mind, He calls us into fellowship. He begins to conform us to the image of His Son and free us from the entanglements of sin and the world. His desire is that we rule over all that is ours. He intends us to govern our person, families, money, fears, and anything that hinders us from knowing and following Christ. The goal is for us to bear "much fruit." It is sobering to think that when we stand before the throne of Christ, one of His measures of judgment will be our fruitfulness. For the sake of His Kingdom in the earth, He is committed to cultivating a people who are predictable, dependable, and consistent.

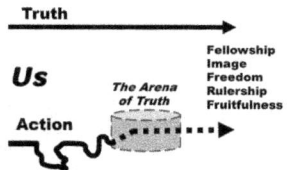

The arena of truth moves us from who we are when we are born again, to who He has predestined us to become[19]. This not an immediate transformation. *This is a journey.* When I powerfully came back to the Lord in the Navy, I thought everything was all straightened out and things would be glorious forever more. All I needed to do was love Jesus. Little did I know the "adventures" He had planned. When we accept the Lord's invitation to follow Him, He says, "Wonderful! Put your head in this yoke with me and we'll start."

Jesus uses the picture of the yoke in Matthew 11:29 as a *relationship of learning*. We learn from Him how to live. When a young ox is being trained, it is put in a double yoke with an older, well-trained ox. As the older ox responds to the driver's directions the younger learns to follow. It is a process. There is no such thing as instant maturity.

> So, Jesus was saying to those Jews who had believed Him, "If you continue in My word, then you are truly disciples of Mine; and you will know the truth, and the truth will make you free." They answered Him, "We are Abraham's descendants and have never yet been enslaved to anyone; how is it that You say, 'You will become free?'" Jesus answered them, "Truly, truly, I say to you, everyone who commits sin is the slave of sin. The slave does not remain

---

19 See Romans 8:28-29.

in the house forever; the son does remain forever. So, if the Son makes you free, you will be free indeed."[20]

Jesus was speaking to those who had "believed in Him." They were not religious antagonists or irreligious law breakers. He was explaining the intended function of the arena of truth:

First, "If you continue in My word,"
Second, "Then you are truly disciples of Mine;"
Third, "And you will know the truth,"
Forth, "And the truth will make you free."

Jesus did not say that knowing truth comes from good teaching or more knowledge of Scripture. The religious Jews searched Scripture for "eternal life" but missed the *Person* who was the source of Life.[21] Jesus said that we attain truth by continuing to walk with Him in the yoke of discipleship. Truth is not just good doctrine. According to Jesus, *truth is a learned behavior.* Walking in truth is aligning our behavior, internally and externally, with the person and pattern of Jesus.

Out of the Father's deep passion for our fellowship and freedom, He confronts us using "all things" in the arena of truth. His purpose is to expose and remove things that hinder us from genuine fellowship and being conformed to the Pattern Son.

20 John 8:31-37
21 See John 5:39-40

But the arena represents conflict, and we don't want to go in there!

We are comfortable with ourselves. When we are in the Arena, we find ourselves having to grapple internally with what the Lord shines His light on. We must wrestle with the light until we embrace God's answer for the situation.

It may work something like this: God begins revealing to you that you are an insensitive and self-centered husband (or wife, or father, or mother). He may start very subtly with little glimpses. Or it may be a dramatic confrontation that's not very pleasant. So, you begin to argue and dodge the issue.

You tell the Lord, "But I really love her!"

He reminds you, "I didn't ask about that. You are insensitive."

"But I gave her a gold American Express card."

"You are missing the point. I said you are insensitive and self-centered. It's not a matter of love or generosity. It's how you conduct yourself as a husband."

Once when I was in a discussion with a man, and he said, "Bob, I really regard you. You're the most wonderful Bible teacher I've ever heard. I want to hear the truth about myself. Lay it on me; tell me like it is."

I really believed he wanted me to. So, I said, "If I've ever seen anybody insensitive to their wife, it is you."

His countenance fell, his color changed, and

steam came out of his ears! For a second, I was afraid he would take a swing at me. He stormed up and down the room like a caged animal. After a while, his blood pressure went down, and tears came to his eyes. Finally, he said "I really find that hard to believe. But because you said it, I'm gonna take it by faith." Out of his response, God healed his home. In the course of a few minutes, I witnessed the man enter the arena of truth, be hit with truth's bitterness, wrestle with it, and embrace it. His bottom line was that he ultimately loved truth more than he loved his pride.

The Lord wants to bring us through the arena of truth to reveal something to us. He longs to work reality into our lives that we might be predictable, dependable, and consistent. Many are inclined to believe that if there is conflict it cannot be God. God is a God of peace, right? If I just rebuke the Devil and quote the Bible long enough, all the conflict will go away. In reality, truth often incites deep, internal conflict. It challenges the comfort zone of our hidden, personal short comings.

My journey of life in the Lord involves two separate arenas. One is my beliefs about God and His ways as I understand Him from Scripture and through many whom I have embraced as mentors. When I came back to the Lord my basic spiritual worldview was Pentecostal with all that was both helpful and limiting. Later the Lord directed me to attend a Reformed Episcopalian seminary, which was based in the theology of Calvinism. Seminary was three years of challenging adjustments as the Lord broadened my understanding. He revealed Himself beyond my Pentecostal theology. My theology was not wrong; it was simply inadequate for where the Lord wanted to take me.

Throughout my life the Holy Spirit has consistently challenged me to embrace new vistas of reality in the pursuit of truth. I have been compelled to adjust myself through the Charismatic renewal, my understanding of the working of demons, the breadth of the work of Christ, the universal governing power of Agape, eschatology, and many other areas of reality.

The second arena, and the more challenging, has been adjustments in my own person. Using other people and circumstances, Father has sought to align me with the truth of His Person. He has exposed motives, attitudes, and habits that were often exceedingly painful to acknowledge. After almost seven decades I cannot say that my "arrow" is absolutely aligned with Christ's, but I am blessed to report that my squiggly line is flatter than it was at the beginning.

As you look at your own arenas, I believe you will find they somewhat match my own. A danger in Western Christianity is imbalance. We tend to pursue greater knowledge of Scripture or the latest "new truth" that we think will advance our personal maturity. Or on the other extreme, we strive for a form of "holiness" or spirituality without regard for the boundaries of Scripture and sound doctrine. I will discuss more on this in the next *Plumbline*.

Responses to the Arena

What happens when we find ourselves facing the conflict of the arena? We have at least five possible responses to the arena. I have observed these over the years and have seen them working in my own person.

1. **Denial**

We deny the truth of the arena is real. Tell someone he is an alcoholic and he will deny it because, "I can quit anytime I want."

A woman feels a growing lump in her breast. She continues to tell herself, "It's nothing; lots of women have lumpy breasts."

I had a policeman friend who caught a young man literally in the act of stealing parts off cars; he was holding hubcaps. The policeman took the young man home and rang the doorbell. His mother answered the door. There her son stood with the hubcaps and other items still in his hands.

The officer looked at his mother and said, "I caught your son stealing these things off of cars."

She looked at her son, then at the officer, and

rather forcefully said, "Don't tell me my son does that. My son would never steal anything. It's you cops. You have no business harassing decent young men."

The officer was so disgusted that he quit the police force. The mother was unwilling to believe that her son was a thief. She denied the reality standing right in front of her.

2. Avoidance

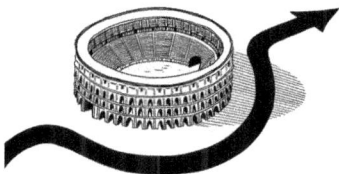

We avoid the arena as a convenient response. I believe avoidance is part of our natural "flight or fight" to a perceived threat. Let me clarify that avoidance, as it is used here, is different from procrastination as we often experience it. I may procrastinate reorganizing my desk drawers or thinning out my closet simply because it is boring, and I have "more important" things to do.

Avoidance of the arena is making a conscious decision not to engage a situation. The situation threatens the potential for painful conflict and the real possibility of a negative outcome. For example, I may choose to avoid being the negative voice in a committee meeting when everyone else is positive. I rationalize thinking, "They really know more than I do." Or "I really don't want to throw cold water on something that looks so good."

Life is filled with situations involving conflict. Demanding an adult child get a job; reporting a co-worker making unwanted sexual suggestions; or insisting a family member repay a loan are all situations we might choose to avoid. Flight is less threatening than fight.

3. Endure Without Change

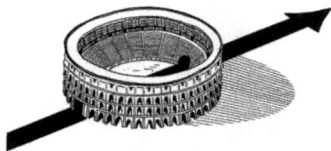

I call this "the white-knuckle club." In the face of conflict, we grip our beliefs, opinions, or habits until our "knuckles turn white." We refuse to yield to truth.

I have watched people be confronted with the same situation time after time and refuse to accept the possibility that something in them might need to yield. They quote more Bible verses, rebuke the Devil, blame someone else, or manipulate the circumstances in order to hold to their position. Somehow, they barely survive each confrontation in the arena.

We need to face and embrace the truth about ourselves. God is offering to bring us freedom. Truth surrounds us, but if we don't embrace change, victory will be an illusion. The great danger is that God will release us to our stubbornness.

In His condemnation of idolatrous Israel, He declared:

Israel is stubborn as a mule. How can God lead him like a lamb to open pasture? Ephraim is addicted to idols. Let him go.[22]

God's desire is to "lead us in green pastures." But we can refuse to follow. In Romans 1:18-32, God's judgment is declared three times as "God gave them over." God allowed them to go their own way, and they reaped the consequences.

4. Turn Back

Turning back is the most painful response to the arena. We face the truth, know with clarity what is required, and decide the price is too high.

Israel made the decision to turn back when they were faced with the arena of overcoming the giants in the Land of Promise. They had the truth of God's promises. They had seen His power in their deliverance from Egypt. Yet, they turned back.

Two things can make us turn back. First, we can be scandalized. This word comes from the

22 Hosea 4:16-17. THE MESSAGE: The Bible in Contemporary Language © 2002 by Eugene H. Peterson

Greek word *skandalizo*, "being caused to stumble." Something becomes too much for us to handle, and we are "tripped up" in our walk. Jesus declared to the Jews, "He who eats My flesh and drinks My blood has eternal life."[23] This was too much for some of His disciples, and they "turned back and no longer followed Him."[24] They were scandalized. Jesus' statement was too much for them to accept.

I have been involved with people who have been painfully confronted with truth. Either directly or by their actions, they asserted, "I can't walk that way anymore. It's just too much. I'm okay just like I am. Jesus is my Savior, my sins are forgiven, and I'm going to heaven. Leave me alone!"

To which I could only answer, "Okay."

Turning back does not mean we don't love Jesus or won't go to Heaven. Our covenantal relationship with the Lord is unchanged, but our fellowship with Him may suffer. Our growth into His image is slowed. We loose a measure of freedom, rulership, and fruitfulness.

The second thing that can make us turn back is rebellion. Paul addressed overt rebellion against truth when he wrote to the Romans concerning humankind:

> For even though they knew God, they did not honor Him as God or give thanks, but they became futile in their speculations,

23 John 6:54.
24 John 6:66, NIV.

and their foolish heart was darkened…
For they exchanged the truth of God
for a lie, and worshiped and served the
creature rather than the Creator, who is
blessed forever. Amen.[25]

It is possible to revolt against truth in spite of
full knowledge and understanding. "They knew
about God but did not honor Him as God." There
can be something inside of us that simply refuses to
hear the voice of the Spirit. Our personal preferences
and fears are crossed. God said of Israel through the
prophet Zechariah:

But they refused to pay attention and
turned a stubborn shoulder and stopped
their ears from hearing. They made their
hearts like flint so that they could not
hear the law and the words which the
Lord of hosts had sent. . . [26]

We all have a latent, powerful potential for
rebellion. We often bury it under what I have termed,
V.R.G., which is verbalized religious garbage.
"That's just the Devil trying to condemn me." "I'm
not under the Law, I'm under grace."

Rebellion, more than any other spiritual response
to truth, opens us to deception and the influence of
the powers of darkness. King Saul rebelled against
the commands of the Lord. As a result, he became

25 Romans 1:21; 25
26 Zechariah 7:11-12

tormented by an evil spirit, consulted with a spirit medium for direction, and finally committed suicide after an ignominious defeat in battle.

Religious exercise is a poor cure for human rebellion; it most often inflames. The true cure is to humbly accept Christ's yoke. We learn to respond like Mary, "Be it unto me according to your word."[27]

5. Embrace and Change

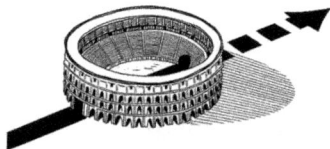

The last and best response to the arena is to embrace the conflict and allow the Spirit of God to change us from the inside out. It is often uncomfortable and possibly painful. We might be tempted to find some other alternative. But in the end, it is the only way to move forward.

One of the keys for hearing what God is saying to you is to recognize that He often sends someone or a circumstance to do the talking. We would like to have God show up in person and just tell us what He wants. He tried that at Mt. Sinai, and it produced a nation of rebels. And when He showed up in the flesh, we crucified Him. The arena may come first as a gentle nudging inviting our attention. If we are incapable of hearing, then tension increases.

For example, you have $25,000 in credit card

27 Luke 1:38

debt. Your accountant warns, "You don't know how to handle money."

You deny the truth, blow him off, and find a new accountant. You go to your new accountant asking for help. You are now upside down with $35,000 in credit card debt and sinking further. Your new accountant tells you the same thing. "You need to learn how to handle money."

It's hard to admit as a 40-year-old adult that you need help learning how to manage money. Are you willing to face truth and do something about your financial habits? You tell your accountant, "You're right. I'll do something about it next year!"

It's easier to avoid it since you can't deny it any longer. However, you can be sure that if you don't embrace the truth and change, you will have to face it again. Next time you will be deeper in the hole than you are now.

Years ago, I felt the Lord inspire me with this little jingle: "If you fix the fix God fixed to fix you, then God will fix another fix to fix you. " Meditate on this, and you will find that it nicely summarizes all I have been trying to present.

My friends in the Lord, especially my wife, tell me, "Bob, you really are a stubborn man."

"Not me," I reply, "I just hold my convictions with firmness." I go through the conflict with white knuckles and refuse to change. The truth is, I'm like an army mule. When I plant my heels, you might as well forget trying to argue with me.

Finally, I acknowledge that if I am going to permit the Lord to conform me to His image, I must allow Him to work me out of stubbornness.

But I whine, "Lord it is so painful! I think I'm going to have a heart attack."

He scolds me, "Grow up. Go into the arena and embrace the truth. Don't try to avoid it, deny it, or run from it. Embrace it, and let Me change you."

At some point we must learn to abandon our claims to personal sovereignty. We can put our heads in the yoke of obedience and move forward by faith in the Father's ultimate love and goodness.

Our journeys through the arena are:

- Father designed,
- Jesus yoked, and
- Spirit empowered.

When we begin to see the results of embracing the arena, certain Scriptures dawn on us with new clarity:

Exalt in tribulation . . . love poured out in our hearts.[28]

Consider it all joy when you encounter various trials . . . perfect and complete lacking in nothing.[29]

In this you greatly rejoice, even though now for a little while, if

28 Romans 5:3-5
29 James 1:2-4.

necessary, you have been distressed
by various trials . . . result in praise,
glory, and honor.[30]

As we begin to align ourselves with the truth,
we start to enjoy that for which we have been
created—fellowship, image, freedom, rulership, and
fruitfulness. We step out of what we are presently,
into what God wants us to become. We journey step
by step, lesson by lesson, truth by truth, and arena
by arena. In the process, we can rejoice knowing He
is the ultimate prize.

Much of the Church wants a "magic wand" faith.
We long for the anointed person to lay hands on us
and command, "Be thou perfect. Temper, be gone!"
We hope to simply speak to the problem and have
it disappear. We are told in a seven-part DVD series
to pray in Jesus' name and be free or to declare a
promise and see it happen.

Does God ever respond in these instances? In
His mercy and grace, He sometimes does. I have
known addicts to be instantly delivered. I have seen
people set free from deep emotional wounds with a
single prayer or a deep experience in the presence
of God's love. We look expectantly to the Lord;
however, most of life requires walking step by step.
Even though He has given unusual gifts of power to
certain individuals, as far as I know, God does not
hand out "magic wands."

---

30 1 Peter 1:6-7.

As we begin to understand our own personal arenas, we do well to remember Alexander Solzhenitsyn's admonition: "Truth eludes us if we do not concentrate our attention totally on its pursuit." He is describing the focus we must develop if we are to successfully engage our own arenas. God is preparing a generation of sons and daughters for the work of the harvest who are predictable, dependable, and consistent.

What's Next

In this *Plumbline*, I have focused on the challenges we face when we encounter truth. We will need this, along with the basic framework of truth outlined in the previous *Plumbline*[31] as a reference in order to have a common understanding as we continue.

In the next *Plumbline,* I will begin to look at the *dynamics of truth.* How does God bring truth to us in history? How do we understand the Scripture to know truth as God wants to present it? These questions will prove to be helpful in our journeys to fellowship, freedom, and fruitfulness.

---

31 The first volume, *The Arena of Truth: Establishing the Borders*, is available at www.lifechangers.org

LIFECHANGERS®

P.O. Box 3709 ❖ Cookeville, TN 38502
931.520.3730 ❖ lc@lifechangers.org

www.ingramcontent.com/pod-product-compliance
Lightning Source LLC
Chambersburg PA
CBHW071754020426
42331CB00008B/2310